Cells and

Holly Wallace

Systems

www.heinemann.co.uk
Visit our website to find out more information about Heinemann Library books.

To order:
 Phone 44 (0) 1865 888066
 Send a fax to 44 (0) 1865 314091
 Visit the Heinemann Bookshop at www.heinemann.co.uk to browse our catalogue and order online.

First published in Great Britain by Heinemann Library,
Halley Court, Jordan Hill, Oxford OX2 8EJ
a division of Reed Educational and Professional Publishing Ltd.
Heinemann is a registered trademark of Reed Educational & Professional Publishing Ltd.

OXFORD MELBOURNE AUCKLAND
JOHANNESBURG BLANTYRE GABORONE
IBADAN PORTSMOUTH (NH) USA CHICAGO

Designed by Celia Floyd
Originated by Dot Gradations
Printed by Wing King Tong, in Hong Kong

ISBN 0 431 10886 2
04 03 02 01 00
10 9 8 7 6 5 4 3 2 1

British Library Cataloguing in Publication Data

Wallace, Holly
  Cells and systems. – (Life processes)
  1. Cells – Juvenile literature 2. Cytology – Juvenile literature
  I. Title
  571.6

Acknowledgements

The Publishers would like to thank the following for permission to reproduce photographs:

Action Plus: Glyn Kirk pg.15; *Science Photo Library*: pg.20, Andrew Syred pg.5, pg.11, Eye of Science pg.6, Claude Nuridsany & Marie Perennou pg.6, CNRI pg.7, Dr Jeremy Burgess pg.10, Manfred Kage pg.12, Prof P Motta/Dept of Anatomy/University La Sapienza/Rome pg.13, pg.25, Profs P Motta, PM Andrews, KR Porter & J Vial pg.14, National Cancer Institute pg.16, Manfred Kage pg.19, D Phillips pg.21, Quest pg.23, Don Wong pg.24, Don Fawcett pg.27, Dr Yorgos Nikas pg.28, Neil Bromhall pg.28, L Willatt/East Anglian Genetics Service pg.29.

Cover photograph reproduced with permission of Science Photo Library.

Every effort has been made to contact copyright holders of any material reproduced in this book. Any omissions will be rectified in subsequent printings if notice is given to the Publisher.

Any words appearing in the text in bold, **like this**, are explained in the glossary.

Contents

Introduction

Cells and Systems looks at the amazing world of plant and animal cells and systems. Every living thing, however small, is made up of cells that form the different parts of its body. In many living things, groups of specialized cells make tissues such as skin or bones. Groups of tissues make organs such as the heart or lungs. Groups of organs work together to form body systems, which carry out the processes and functions of a living thing.

What are cells?

All living things are made up of cells. A cell is a tiny unit of living material that is the basic building block of life. Cells are like tiny factories where chemical reactions happen. These reactions keep living things alive and in good working order. Plant and animal cells do similar jobs, such as taking in food, releasing energy and getting rid of waste, but there are some differences in their structures.

Did you know?
Your body is made up of some 50 billion (million million) cells. The largest human cells are female egg cells, or ova, which measure 0.1 millimetres across and can just be seen with the naked eye. (Most cells can only be seen under a microscope.) The smallest cells are in your brain and measure just 0.005 millimetres across.

Animal cells

An animal cell is like a tiny, jelly-filled bag, held together by a thin, outer 'skin' called a **membrane**. In the centre is the **nucleus**, which controls everything that happens inside the cell. The diagram shows the main parts of a typical animal cell.

A typical animal cell.

Cell membrane – The cell's outer 'skin', which holds the cell together. It allows food and **oxygen** into the cell and waste products made in the cell out of it.

Cytoplasm – A jelly-like substance that fills most of the cell and is mostly made of **protein** and water. This is where the chemical reactions happen that keep the cell alive.

Nucleus – The control centre of the cell. It contains chemical instructions that tell the cell what to do. The nucleus also divides to make new cells for growth, repair and **reproduction**.

Plant cells

Plant cells have all the same features as animal cells but have three extra ones. These are a tough, rigid cell wall made of a substance called **cellulose**, chloroplasts for making food and a large, permanent vacuole filled with cell **sap**. Here you can see the main parts of a typical plant cell.

A typical plant cell.

Cytoplasm

Nucleus

Cell wall – A rigid wall around the outside of the cell. It is made of tough fibres of cellulose that support the cell and give it its shape.

Vacuole – A large space inside the cell that is filled with cell sap. This is a watery fluid containing dissolved **minerals** and food.

Chloroplasts – Tiny structures that give plants their green colour. They contain a green chemical called **chlorophyll** which plants use to help them make their own food.

How many cells?

Some living things, such as human beings and trees, are made up of millions of cells. They are called multi-cellular, or many-celled, **organisms**. Other living things consist of only one cell. They are called uni-cellular, or single-celled, organisms. The amoeba is a tiny, uni-cellular organism that lives in water. Its cytoplasm flows along to make it move and it feeds by engulfing its prey. To reproduce, an amoeba simply divides in two.

An amoeba is a uni-cellular organism.

Cell specialists

Cells make up every part of a living thing, but not all cells look the same. You are made up of many different types of cells. For example, the cells that make your bones, nerves, or muscles, have special features to help them to do a particular job. Cells do not work on their own, but are grouped together to build the different parts of your body.

Specialized cells

Cells come in different shapes and sizes, depending on the job they do. They are called 'specialized', which means that they can only carry out one type of work. Here are some examples of specialized cells:

- Nerve cells – Nerve cells, or **neurones**, have long, thin fibres for carrying messages all over your body (see page 27).
- Red blood cells – Red blood cells carry **oxygen** around your body. They are doughnut shaped to give a large surface area for picking up as much oxygen as possible (see page 16).
- Ciliated epithelial cells – Flattened cells that form a thin layer to line your air passages. They are covered in tiny hairs called **cilia** that trap harmful dirt and germs (see page 21).
- Root hair cells – A plant's roots suck up vital water and **minerals** from the ground. The roots are covered in long, hair-like cells that provide a large surface area for taking in water.

Tiny cells called cilia line your air passages.

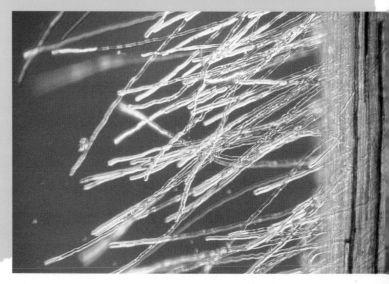

Plant root-hairs.

Cells and systems

Groups of specialized cells make tissues, such as your muscle or bone tissue. Groups of different tissues make organs, such as your heart or lungs. A group of organs working together is called a system, such as your digestive system. This uses various organs, such as your intestines and stomach. All the systems work together to form an **organism**, such as you!

Life processes

The cells in your body work together to keep you alive. They carry out the seven life processes, which are:

1 Movement – All living things can move their bodies.
2 Respiration – This is how cells use oxygen to release energy from food.
3 Sensitivity – All living things sense and respond to changes in the outside world.
4 Feeding – All living things need food for energy and growth.
5 Excretion – All living things must get rid of waste products from their bodies.
6 **Reproduction** – Living things produce young to replace those that die.
7 Growth – All living things grow. Most animals grow until they reach adult size. Some plants never stop growing.

Did you know?

Some of the cells in your body last throughout your life and others only live for a few days. When they die, they are replaced with new cells. Some of your brain cells will last a lifetime, your bone cells will last for about 30 years, but the cells that line your small intestine only live for two to three days.

Brain cells.

Plant systems

Plants range from tiny, single-celled **algae** to towering trees, made of many millions of cells. Most plant cells follow the basic pattern shown on page 5, but some are specialized for particular jobs, such as making food, taking in water or carrying water around the plant. Groups of plant cells work together to form tissues, such as xylem and phloem (explained on pages 10 and 11). Groups of different tissues form organs, such as the plant's roots, stems and leaves.

Parts of a plant

Flowering plants range from daisies and grasses to huge horse chestnut trees. These plants look very different from each other but they all have a similar structure.

Leaves – Cells inside the leaves contain **chlorophyll**, which absorbs sunlight for **photosythesis. Veins** in the leaves carry food and water around the plant.

Flowers – These contain the plant's sex cells for **reproduction**.

Stem – The stem supports the plant and holds the leaves up to the sunlight. It also carries food and water up and down the plant.

Roots – The roots anchor the plant in the ground and take in water and **minerals**.

A plant's systems are all basically the same, whether a small flower or a huge tree.

Making food

All living things need energy to survive. This energy comes from their food. Green plants make their own food by photosynthesis. This takes place in the plant's leaf cells, inside tiny, disc-shaped structures called chloroplasts. The chloroplasts contain a green chemical called chlorophyll. It uses energy from sunlight to turn carbon dioxide from the air and water from the ground into a sugary food called **glucose**.

Respiration

To release energy from the glucose, plants use **oxygen** from the air. This is called **respiration** and it happens inside the plant's cells. The plants take in oxygen through their leaves and give off carbon dioxide as waste. Respiration also continues throughout the night when the plant cannot photosynthesize.

Flower functions

Flowers contain a plant's male parts, which produce **pollen** (the male sex cells), and female parts, which produce **ovules** (the female sex cells). For a new plant to grow, pollen must travel from the male to the female parts. This is called **pollination**. Then the **nuclei** of the pollen and ovule fuse, or join together, to make a new cell. This is called **fertilization**. The new cell grows into a seed that contains a new plant and a store of food.

Inside a leaf

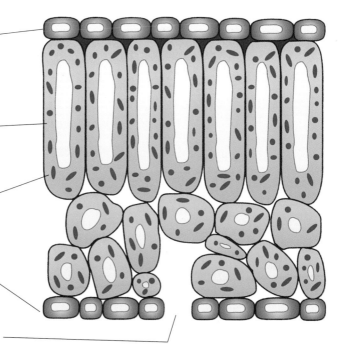

Upper epidermis – This is the upper skin of the leaf. It is made up of a single layer of transparent cells that allow sunlight to pass through to the palisade cells.

Palisade cells – This is a layer of tall, column-like cells that are found just under the upper epidermis where they receive most light.

Chloroplasts – These are found in the **cytoplasm** of the palisade cells. They contain chlorophyll for photosynthesis.

Lower epidermis – This is the lower skin of the leaf.

Stomata – These are tiny holes in the leaf for allowing water and gases in and out (see page 11).

Plant plumbing

Inside a plant, specialized cells work together to carry food and water around the plant in a constant flow. The water is sucked up from the ground through the plant's root system and carried up the stem to the plant's leaves.

Root hair cells

A plant's roots grow downwards and sideways into the ground. Their tips are covered in thousands of tiny, tube-like structures, called root-hairs. These are actually formed from the root's outer cells. They grow between the particles of soil and absorb water and **minerals** by **osmosis** (explained opposite). Having so many root-hairs greatly increases the roots' surface area so they can take in more water.

A plant's roots are covered in root-hairs.

Transport system

From the roots, the water is carried up the plant to the leaves through a system of tiny tubes called xylem. Another set of tubes, called phloem, carry food in the form of sticky **sap** from the leaves to the rest of the plant. All these tubes form the plant's 'plumbing system'. The xylem and phloem are arranged in bundles running through the plant's stem, like bundles of tiny drinking straws. Xylem and phloem are called **vascular tissue**. Some simple, non-flowering plants, such as mosses and **algae**, do not have vascular tissue.

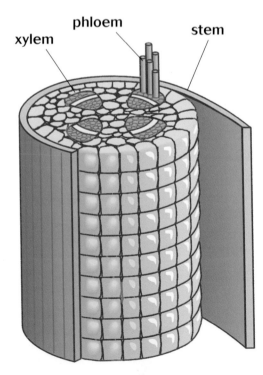

Inside a plant stem.

What is osmosis?

Water enters a plant's roots by osmosis. This is the way water moves from one cell to another. Some cells contain concentrated cell sap, with a large amount of **glucose** dissolved in a small amount of water. Others contain much weaker sap. In osmosis, water moves from the weak sap to the strong. Root-hairs draw in water by osmosis because their cell sap is stronger than the water in the soil.

Did you know?

The wood in a tree trunk is made up of old xylem tubes. As the tree grows, the tubes of dead xylem cells in the centre of the trunk fill with a hard, woody material called lignin. This supports the trunk and the tree's great weight. The younger, outer layer of xylem still carries water through the plant.

Losing water

Some of the water drawn up through the plant is used in **photosynthesis**. But most of it is lost through tiny holes on the underside of the leaves. The water then **evaporates** from the leaves into the air. These holes are called stomata. Each stoma (the singular of stomata) is surrounded by two sausage-shaped guard cells, (you can see them clearly in the picture) which open and close the stoma.

Stomata on a rose leaf.

11

Bones

Like plants, all animals, including you, are made up of cells. Your body is like a complicated machine, with many different parts. Your cells, tissues, organs and systems all work together to make you grow and keep you healthy, and to keep your body machine in good working order. Like plant cells, many of the cells in your body are specialized to do a particular job. Take the bones in your skeleton, for example.

Skeleton support

Your skeleton is made up of a system of bones inside your body and it has three important jobs to do. Firstly, it acts like the framework of beams and girders inside a building to hold your body up and give it its shape. Without a skeleton, your body would simply collapse in a heap. Secondly, your skeleton protects the organs of your body from being bumped or knocked. For example, your bony skull protects your delicate brain. Thirdly, your bones anchor your muscles so that you can move about (see page 14).

The human skeleton acts as support and protection for the body.

12

Tough bones

Because of all the jobs it must do, bone tissue is highly specialized. The outer part of a bone is made of tough, non-living tissue. It is mainly **minerals**, such as **calcium**. It is extremely strong for supporting your body weight and absorbing bumps and knocks. The inside of the bone is living tissue that is soft and spongy. This makes bones light so that you can move about, and flexible so that they do not snap or break too easily. In old age, people's bones have less living tissue so they become brittle and are easily broken. Some of the larger bones in your body contain a soft tissue called **marrow**. This makes your red blood cells (see page 16).

Growing bones

There are more than 200 bones in your skeleton. They come in a wide range of shapes and sizes, but they all have the same basic structure. When you were a baby, some of your cells formed tough, gristly **cartilage**. Gradually, the cartilage 'ossified', or turned into hard bone. This process will carry on until you are about 25 years old. Some of the cartilage never turns to bone. You can still feel cartilage, for example, in the end of your nose and in your ear flaps.

The spongy tissue inside a bone.

Did you know?

Your bones are covered in a thin, tough, outer layer of living bone cells called the periosteum. If you break a bone, cells in the periosteum divide and multiply, and grow over the break, joining the broken parts together. You might need a plaster cast to help the bones heal straight.

Moving muscles

There are hundreds of muscles all over your body – in your organs, such as your heart and bladder, or attached between your bones to allow you to move. Your muscles are a type of tissue. The muscles that cover your skeleton are known as stripy muscles because they look stripy under a microscope. The muscles in your organs are called smooth muscles. Smooth muscles work all the time, automatically. They are what make you breathe. A special muscle called **cardiac** muscle keeps your heart beating.

Stripy muscle fibres.

Muscle cells

Stripy muscle tissue is made up of bundles of long, thin, thread-like cells, which are usually called muscle fibres. There are more than 2000 fibres inside a large muscle. Each fibre is made up of even finer threads, called myofibrils. Muscle fibres can be up to 30 centimetres long. Their long, thin shape allows them to stretch so that you can move the different parts of your body. The whole muscle is covered in a protective, elastic 'skin' called the epimysium.

How muscles work

Muscles are attached to your bones by strong straps called **tendons**. Muscles pull on your bones to make them move. When you want to move your arm, for example, your brain sends electrical signals to your muscles, telling the fibres to contract, or become shorter. This gives a pulling force. Muscles can only pull, not push, so most of your muscles work in pairs. In your upper arm, for example, the biceps muscle contracts to bend your elbow. Then it relaxes and its partner, the triceps, contracts to straighten your arm.

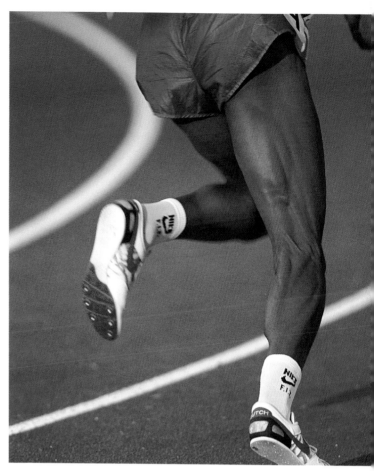

The clearly defined, stripy muscles of a sprinter.

Muscle power

Your muscles need a constant supply of **oxygen** and energy from food to keep them working properly. These are carried to your muscles in your blood, through tiny blood vessels that are wrapped around each bundle of muscle fibres. If supplies of oxygen and energy run low but your muscles are still working hard, they may go into a painful spasm. This is known as cramp.

Did you know?

You have more than 600 muscles in your body. The largest are in your thighs and bottom and are called the gluteus maximus muscles. Your smallest muscles are attached to the tiny bones deep inside your ears. They are called the stapedius muscles and are about the size of a pinhead.

The circulatory system

Your cells need energy from food and **oxygen** from the air to keep them working properly. These are carried around your body by your blood, through blood vessels. Your blood also collects waste products for disposal. Pumped along by your heart, your blood circulates continuously around your body. Your heart, blood and blood vessels make up your circulatory system.

Blood cells

Blood is made up of a clear, straw-coloured liquid called plasma. Floating in it are red blood cells, white blood cells and platelets. You have about 5 litres of blood.

- Plasma – Plasma is made up of water in which **proteins**, salts, food and waste materials are dissolved.
- Red blood cells – Red blood cells carry oxygen from your lungs. They are made in the jelly-like **marrow** inside your large bones. Red blood cells contain a chemical called **haemoglobin**. This is what makes blood red. It absorbs oxygen in your lungs, then your blood flows to your heart to be pumped around your body.
- White blood cells – White blood cells help your body to fight disease. Some eat up harmful germs, which enter your body through cuts, food or in the air. Others make chemicals called **antibodies**. They stick on to germs and kill them.
- Platelets – Platelets are tiny fragments of cells that have broken off larger cells in the bone marrow. They help your blood to clot so that you do not lose too much when you cut yourself.

Red blood cells, white blood cells and platelets all float in the plasma in your blood.

Blood vessels

Blood travels in tubes called blood vessels. You have so many of these that, put end to end, they would stretch more than twice around the Earth. **Arteries** are strong, muscular tubes that carry blood from your heart. They divide into tiny **capillaries** that reach your body cells. The walls of the capillaries are only one cell thick so that substances can easily pass between them and your cells. The capillaries join up again to form **veins**, which return the blood to your heart.

The circulatory system of the human body.

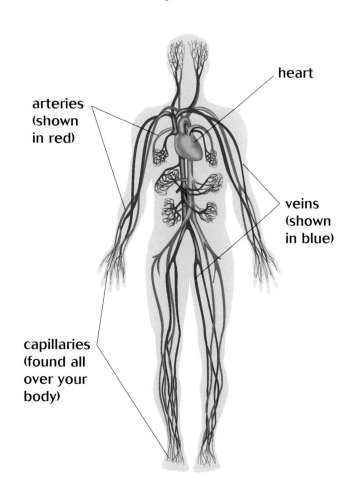

heart

arteries (shown in red)

veins (shown in blue)

capillaries (found all over your body)

The heart

Your heart is an organ. It works like a pump, pushing blood around your body. It pumps, or beats, about once every second and, with each beat, sends blood surging along the arteries. Your heart is made of strong **cardiac** muscle. As the muscle contracts, it squeezes blood out and around your body. Each contraction is called a heartbeat. During exercise, your heart has to beat faster to supply your muscles with extra energy. Your **pulse** rate measures how often your heart beats per minute.

Did you know?

A pin-prick of blood contains an amazing 2,500,000 red blood cells, 5000 white blood cells and 250,000 platelets. In total, you have about 30 billion red blood cells in your body, more than any other type of cell.

The digestive system

Everything you do uses energy. Walking and running use lots of energy. But breathing, blinking and even standing still use energy too. You get this energy from the food you eat. Food also supplies all the chemicals you need for growth and to keep your body working properly. The useful parts of food are carried to your cells by your blood. But only tiny **molecules** of food can pass into your blood, so first, the food must be broken down. This happens as it passes through your body and travels along your digestive system. This is called **digestion**.

Digesting a meal

1 Your teeth and tongue chew and mash your food. It is mixed with **saliva** so it is easier to swallow.
2 The food goes down your **oesophagus** into your stomach. It is pushed along by the smooth muscles of the oesophagus walls.
3 In your stomach, the food is mixed with digestive juices that contain special **enzymes**. It forms a creamy mixture.
4 The food passes into the first part of your small intestine. A green liquid, called **bile**, that is made in your liver breaks down any fat into tiny droplets. Other enzymes, made in your **pancreas**, break down the food even more.
5 In the second part of the small intestine, called the ileum the digested food is absorbed into your blood.
6 Any undigested food goes into your large intestine and is passed out of your body as solid waste called **faeces**.

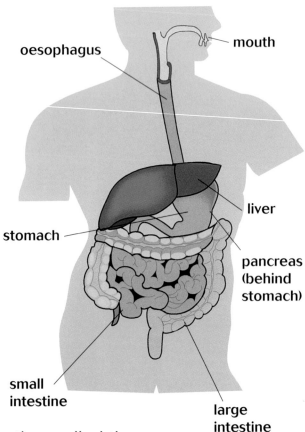

The digestive system.

mouth
oesophagus
liver
stomach
pancreas (behind stomach)
small intestine
large intestine

How food gets into your blood

The inner wall of the ileum is covered in tiny, finger-like structures called villi. These make a huge surface area for absorbing food. The villi walls are only one cell thick so that food can pass easily through them and into tiny blood vessels that carry it around your body to your cells.

Finger-like villi cover the wall of the small intestine.

Speedy enzymes

Enzymes are special chemicals made in your cells. They are called catalysts, which means that they can speed up the chemical reactions taking place in your body. There are thousands of different types of enzymes. Digestive enzymes help to break down and dissolve your food as it passes through your digestive system.

Did you know?

Your digestive system is about 9 metres long and a meal takes about three days to pass through. Your small intestine alone measures about 6 metres long. It is only called 'small' because it is not very wide.

The respiratory system

Your body needs **oxygen** to release the energy from the food. When you breathe in, you take air into your lungs. Here the oxygen is removed and carried to all the cells in your body by your blood. Inside the cells, it is used to release energy from food to keep your cells alive and working. Waste **carbon dioxide** and water are made by your cells. These leave your body when you breathe out. This whole process is called **respiration**. It is easy to confuse 'respiration' with 'breathing', but breathing is only part of the whole process of respiration. It describes the first action, where you take air into your lungs, and the last action, where you breathe carbon dioxide out of them.

Inside a healthy human lung.

Breathing in

When you breathe in, air is sucked in through your nose or mouth. It goes down a large tube called your **trachea** and into two tubes called bronchi that lead into your lungs. The bronchi gradually divide to form a network of tiny tubes, called the bronchioles, like the branches of a tree. As you breathe in, your chest muscles move up and out to let your chest expand so that your lungs can fill with air.

The respiratory system.

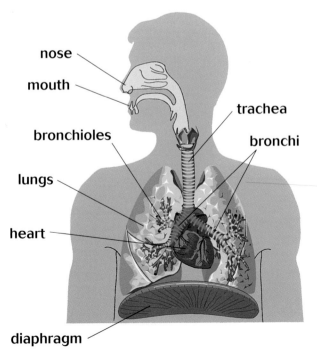

nose
mouth
bronchioles
lungs
heart
trachea
bronchi
diaphragm

Gas exchange

At the end of the smallest branches are bunches of tiny air sacs called alveoli. When you breathe in, these fill with air like tiny balloons. The alveoli are covered with very fine blood vessels. In places, their walls are only one cell thick. Oxygen from the air passes through the walls and into your blood. Then it is carried around your body to your cells where it is used to release energy. You have millions of alveoli in each lung, giving a huge surface area for absorbing oxygen from the air you breathe.

Breathing out

Your blood also carries waste carbon dioxide from your cells to your lungs to be breathed out. It passes from the blood through the walls of the alveoli and into your lungs. Then it is drawn up through your bronchi and trachea, and out through your nose or mouth. When you breathe out, your chest muscles relax. This lowers your chest and raises your **diaphragm**. This reduces the space in your chest, forcing the air out of your lungs.

The alveoli inside a lung are like tiny air sacs.

Did you know?

Two special types of cells line your air passages. One type is covered in tiny hairs called **cilia**. The other produces slimy **mucus**. Dust and germs stick to the mucus, and then the cilia 'beat' it to the back of your mouth so that you can swallow it and clear the germs away. People who smoke often suffer from painful breathing diseases such as **bronchitis**. This is because the chemicals in cigarette smoke prevent the cilia from doing their job properly.

Water and waste

All the chemical processes happening in your cells make waste products, such as **carbon dioxide**, undigested food, and water. All of these must be removed from your body so that they do not harm your cells. You breathe out carbon dioxide (see page 21) during **respiration**, and get rid of waste food as **faeces** (see page 18). You lose waste water when you sweat or **urinate**. Your body is about two-thirds water, which must be kept balanced for your cells to function properly. If you take in more water than you need, your kidneys make **urine** to get rid of the excess liquid and other waste products.

The urinary system

Your kidneys and bladder are known as your urinary system because they make and store urine. Your two kidneys are in your lower back, level with your waist. As blood passes through them, the kidneys filter out waste water and other substances. This waste liquid is called urine. It flows down two tubes, called ureters, into your bladder, an organ that is like a stretchy, muscular bag. The urine is stored in your bladder until you go to the toilet. Then it passes out of your body through a long tube called the urethra.

The urinary system filters out waste and excess water.

kidneys

ureters

bladder

urethra

Did you know?

Filter system

Each kidney contains over a million tiny filtering units called nephrons. Blood flows into your kidneys through your **renal artery**. When it has been cleaned, the blood flows out through your renal **vein** and continues to circulate around your body.

The tiny filters called nephrons inside a kidney.

Poison control

Your liver is the largest organ in your body, weighing over 1.5 kilograms. It does several very important jobs. When your blood has absorbed digested food, it makes a detour through your liver. Your liver stores some of the **nutrients** in the food and changes others into more useful forms. It also gets rid of the toxic, or poisonous, substances found in some food and drink, by turning them into harmless substances. This process is called detoxification.

Your senses

Your five senses are sight, hearing, smell, taste and touch. They tell you about the outside world. You receive information through special **sensory** nerve cells called **receptors**. They react to changes in light or sound, for example, and send messages to your brain. There, the information is processed and your brain tells you what is happening. Many receptors are grouped to form sense organs, such as your eyes, ears or nose.

Eyes and seeing

You see things because light from an object enters your eyes. It is focused by the cornea and lens (see diagram below) to project a sharp, upside-down image onto the retina. Millions of light-sensitive cells on the retina react to the light and send messages to your brain. It interprets the signals and produces the picture you see.

A cross-section of a human-eye.

iris – the coloured part of the eye

pupil – light enters here

lens – focuses the image

cornea – helps focus the image and protect the eye

muscles – move the eye about

retina – area with nerve cells

optic nerve – main nerve to brain

Did you know?

The light-sensitive receptor cells in the retinas of your eyes are called rods and cones. You have about 120 million rods and 7 million cones in each eye. Rods detect black and white, and light intensity. Cones detect colours. Some people are colour blind and cannot see certain colours properly, which means they have faulty cone cells.

The human retina.

24

Ears and hearing

Sounds are vibrations, or waves, in the air. Your earflaps funnel them down your ear canal to the eardrum. This is a thin **membrane** that vibrates as the sound waves hit it. The vibrations are passed on to three tiny bones, then onto another membrane, and then to the **cochlea**. This is filled with liquid that also vibrates. Special nerve cells detect the vibrations and turn them into signals, which travel to your brain. Here they are turned into the sounds that you hear.

Sound-sensitive cells inside an ear.

Taste buds on the surface of the tongue.

Taste and smell

Your tongue and nose are your organs of taste and smell. Your tongue is covered in taste buds, which are lined with taste-sensitive cells. They can detect four main tastes – sweet, salty, sour and bitter. Smells are chemicals floating in the air. They travel up your nose and are picked up by smell receptor cells. Taste and smell are closely linked. If you have a cold and your nose is blocked, you may find it difficult to taste your food.

Skin and touch

Millions of sense receptors are packed beneath the surface of your skin and each type detects a different sensation. Some are sensitive to touch, temperature and pressure. Some tell you if the things you feel are rough, smooth, hard or soft. Other receptors detect pain, which warns you that something is wrong with your body.

Nervous system

Your brain, nerves and **spinal cord** form your body's central nervous system. This processes the information your senses receive about the outside world, and instructs your body how to think, feel or react. Your nerves are like long, fine wires, carrying messages in the form of electrical signals between your brain and other parts of your body. Your spinal cord acts as the main pathway for these messages to travel along. Then your nerves branch out from it to carry the messages all over your body.

Your amazing brain

Your brain controls every part of your body, and everything that you think, learn, remember and feel. It has up to 10,000 million nerve cells, or **neurones**. Nerves carry information about the outside world from your senses to your brain, where it is sorted and processed. Then your brain sends messages along your nerves to your body to tell you what action, if any, to take.

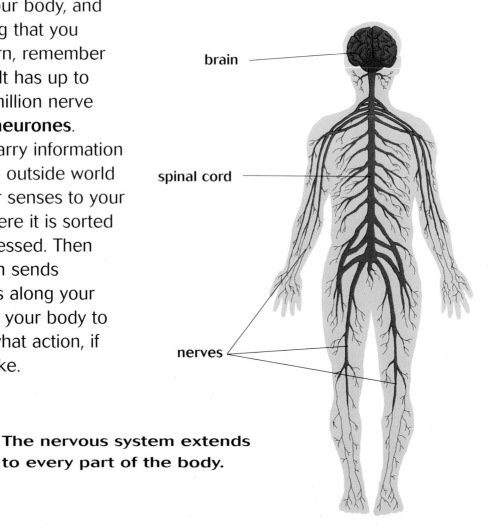

brain

spinal cord

nerves

The nervous system extends to every part of the body.

Nerve cells

A nerve is made up of bunches of long fibres, called axons, which run from the cell bodies of the neurones. Shorter fibres, called dendrites, also branch off from the cell bodies. You have a vast network of about 100 billion (million million) neurones running throughout your body. There are two main types of neurone. **Sensory** neurones carry messages from your sensory organs (see pages 24 to 25) to your central nervous system. **Motor** neurones carry messages from your central nervous system to your muscles to make them move.

How nerves work

One neurone's axons lie very close to the next neurone's dendrites, but they do not actually touch. Nerve signals pass from one neurone to another by 'jumping' over a tiny gap called a synapse. To cross the gap, the signals must change from electrical signals into chemicals called neurotransmitters. Once they have crossed, they turn back into electrical signals again. One neurone has synapses with many other neurones. This means that it can receive many different electrical signals.

A synapse, or nerve junction.

Did you know?

Some of the neurones in your body will last a lifetime but not all of them. Thousands of your brain and nerve cells die every day. In fact, you start losing them even before you are born. Unlike many other types of cells, neurones can never be repaired or replaced, but fortunately, you have millions more so you will never run out!

Reproduction

Reproduction means the creation of new life. Human beings produce sexually, which means that there are two parents who each make sex cells. Male sex cells are called sperm. Female sex cells are called ova, or eggs. For a baby to develop, a sperm must join with an ovum to form a new cell. This is called **fertilization**.

The first cell division of a fertilized egg.

Reproductive systems

Your reproductive system starts working at **puberty**. This usually begins at the age of 11–13 for girls and 12–14 for boys. An ovum is made ready in one of a female's two **ovaries**. It then travels down a tube, called the Fallopian tube. If it meets a sperm cell, it may be fertilized. Sperm cells are made in a male's **testes**. They swim along two tiny tubes, called sperm ducts, to his **penis**.

Male and female

A baby develops when a sperm meets and joins with an ovum in the female's body. This happens when a male and female have sex (sexual intercourse). After fertilization, the two cells make one new cell. This begins to divide until it forms a ball of cells. Then it embeds itself in the female's uterus, or womb. Over the next nine months, it grows and develops into a baby.

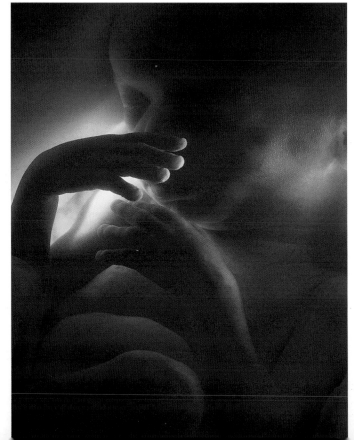

28 **A baby growing inside its mother's womb.**

Cell instructions

Each sex cell carries instructions called genes. Genes are like chemical codes that say what a living thing is and what it looks like. They determine the characteristics you inherit from your parents, such as hair and eye colour. They are carried on very fine threads of material, called chromosomes, inside the **nuclei** of your cells. You inherit 23 chromosomes from each parent. The chromosomes that determine your sex are X and Y chromosomes. All ova carry X chromosomes. Half the sperm carry X chromosomes and half carry Y. If two X chromosomes join, the baby will be a girl. If an X and a Y chromosome join, the baby will be a boy.

Cell division

For a living thing to grow bigger, new cells must be made. Most cells reproduce by splitting in two. There are two types of cell division:

- Mitosis – The nucleus splits in two, forming two new 'daughter' cells. Each of these cells has a full set of chromosomes. The two cells are identical. This type of division is used for growth and repair.
- Meiosis – The nucleus splits in two, forming two new 'daughter' cells. But each of these cells has only half the total number of chromosomes of its parent cell. The two cells are not identical. This type of division is used to produce sex cells for reproduction.

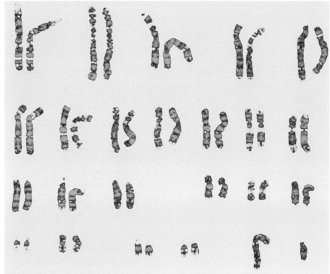

Male chromosomes.

Conclusion

Cells are the building blocks of life, from tiny, single-celled **organisms** to huge, branching trees. Your own body is made of millions of cells. Without cells and the systems that they form, plants would not have green leaves or flowers. You would not be able to move, eat and digest food, or read this book. Everything you take for granted is down to your amazing cells.

Glossary

algae very simple plants found in both saltwater and freshwater

antibodies chemicals made by some types of white blood cells – antibodies stick on to germs and kill them

arteries blood vessels that carry blood away from your heart

bile thick green liquid made in your liver that breaks down fats in your food

bronchitis chest infection that makes breathing difficult and painful

calcium mineral that is essential for building your bones

capillaries smallest blood vessels

carbon dioxide gas that living things breathe out as waste during respiration – plants use carbon dioxide in photosynthesis

cardiac to do with the heart

cartilage rubbery, flexible tissue

cellulose tough material made of fibres found in plant cell walls

chlorophyll green pigment (colouring) found inside plant cells that absorbs energy from sunlight for use in photosynthesis

cilia tiny hair-like structures that cover some cells

cochlea curled tube, filled with liquid, in the inner ear – sound waves shake the liquid which pulls on nerve endings to send signals to the brain

cytoplasm the jelly like substance that fills cells

diaphragm muscle under your chest that contracts and relaxes so you can breathe in and out

digestion way in which food is broken down and processed as it passes through your body

enzymes chemicals made in your cells – some enzymes help break down your food during digestion

evaporate when a liquid, like water, turns into gas

faeces solid waste you pass when you go to the toilet

fertilization joining together of a male and female sex cell to produce a new living thing

glucose a simple sugar – organisms store food as glucose

haemoglobin a chemical in your blood that makes it look red and carries oxygen around your body

marrow jelly-like substance inside some of your larger bones that makes new red and white blood cells

membrane thin sheet of tissue

minerals substances that help to build your body and keep it healthy

molecules tiny particles of a substance

motor motor neurones are nerve cells that carry messages from your brain to your muscles

mucus slimy substance that helps protect the lining of your nose, lungs and stomach

neurones nerve cells

nucleus a rounded structure inside a cell that is the cell's control centre – nuclei is the plural of nucleus

nutrients substances in food that your body needs to function

oesophagus   large tube in your throat through which you swallow food (also called the gullet)

organisms   scientific word for living things

osmosis   the way in which fluid and chemicals pass from one cell to another

ovaries   part of a female's reproductive system – the two ovaries make egg cells

ovules   female sex cells of a plant – after fertilization, they become seeds

oxygen   a gas – all living things need to take in oxygen to survive

pancreas   group of cells (organ) that is part of your digestive system – the pancreas makes enzymes that help break down your food

penis   part of a male's reproductive system – during sexual intercourse, sperm cells swim down the penis into the female's body

photosynthesis   process by which green plants make their own food from carbon dioxide and water, using energy from sunlight absorbed by their chlorophyll

pollen   tiny grains that are the male sex cells of plants

pollination   transfer of pollen from a male flower to a female flower, or from male to female parts of a flower

protein   chemical substance that living things use for growth

puberty   time in a girl or boy's life when their bodies change from being a child to being an adult

pulse   the beats of your heart – you can feel a pulse in your wrist or neck

receptors   special nerve cells that sense the outside world and send messages about it to your brain

renal   to do with the kidneys

reproduction   creation of new life

respiration   the way you breathe in oxygen, used to release energy from your food, and breathe out carbon dioxide as waste

saliva   liquid made in your mouth that helps to break down your food

sap   liquid inside a plant that carries food and water

sensory   sensory neurones are nerve cells that carry messages from your sense organs to your brain

spinal cord   thick bundle of nerves running down your back, inside your spine or backbone

tendons   thick straps of tissue that connect muscles to bones

testes   part of a male's reproductive system where sperm cells are made

trachea   long tube running down your throat used in breathing (also called your windpipe)

urinate   to pass urine when you go to the toilet

urine   liquid you pass out of your body that contains excess water and other waste substances

vascular tissue   the system which carries sap around the plant (made of xylem and phloem)

veins   **1)** tiny tubes in a leaf that carry food and water **2)** vessels that carry blood back to your heart

Index